D1708306

About this book

Can you imagine what it was like to grow up in the Middle Ages? Every page in this book shows you something about the children who lived all those years ago. You can watch medieval children going to school, playing games and taking part in sports. Some of the games are quite like those you play today.

Most children did not go to school at all. Boys from rich families often went to a nearby castle to become a page in the lord's service. At the castle they learned to ride, fence and joust, so that one day they could become knights. Other boys were apprenticed to master-craftsmen and learned a trade such as weaving, tailoring or printing. Girls usually stayed at home and were taught by their mothers to sew and embroider, to cook and look after the house. Look carefully at the pictures in this book, and you will find out a great deal about how children lived more than five hundred years ago.

Some of the words printed in *italics* may be new to you. You can look them up in the word list on page 92.

AN EYEWITNESS BOOK

Growing Up
in the
Middle Ages

PENELOPE DAVIES

More Eyewitness Books

The Railway Builders Alistair Barrie
Pirates and Buccaneers Tilla Brading
The Mayflower Pilgrims Brenda Colloms
The Age of Drake Leonard Cowie
Children of the Industrial Revolution Penelope Davies
Country Life in the Middle Ages Penelope Davies
Growing up in the Middle Ages Penelope Davies
Canals Jane Dorner
Markets and Fairs Jane Dorner
Newgate to Tyburn Jane Dorner
Kitchens and Cooking Kathy & Mike Eldon
The Story of the Cinema Helen du Feu
The Story of the Wheel Peter Hames
Men in the Air Roger Hart
Popular Entertainment Elizabeth Holt
A Victorian Sunday Jill Hughes
Livingstone in Africa Denis Judd
Stage Coach and Highwayman Stephanie McKnight
The Tudor Family Ann Mitchell
The Horseless Carriage Lord Montagu
The Firefighters Ann Mountfield
The Slave Trade Ann Mountfield
Clothes in History Angela Schofield
Florence Nightingale Philippa Stewart
Sport through the Ages Peter Wilson
The Glorious Age of Charles II Helen Wodzicka
Ships and Seafarers Helen Wodzicka
The Printer and his Craft Helen Wodzicka
The Voyages of Captain Cook Roger Hart
Town Life in the Middle Ages Penelope Davies
Road Transport Susan Goldblatt
Shops and Shopping Ann Mountfield
Shakespeare and his Theatre Philippa Stewart
Tutankhamun's Egypt Philippa Stewart
The Story of Medicine Kathy & Mike Eldon
Tom-tom to Television Kathy & Mike Eldon
Toys in History Angela Schofield

Frontispiece: An apprentice blacksmith shows his skill to a noble lady.

First published 1972
Second impression 1975
Third impression 1979
ISBN 85340 174 8

Copyright © 1972 by
Wayland Publishers Ltd
49 Lansdowne Place Hove, Sussex BN3 1HF
Printed and bound in Great Britain at The Pitman Press, Bath

Contents

Home Life

Children grew up in very small houses in the *Middle Ages*. Most homes only had one room with a fireplace in the centre. Here, the whole family ate, slept and relaxed. Not until Henry IV's reign (1399–1413) were bigger houses built, mainly in the towns.

Parents in those days were very strict with their children. In the early 1400s Agnes Paston beat her daughter at least once a week. Many mothers did the same. People used to say, "The more a father loves his child, the more busily he beats him." Children grew up much quicker than they do today. They were expected to behave as adults when they were in their early teens. One reason was that people did not live so long. Not many people lived to be fifty.

People also married when they were much younger. When King Richard II (1377–99) married his first wife, he was only sixteen. After she died, he married Isabella, daughter of the French king. He was nineteen, but she was only seven! Marriage between very young children was often arranged for political reasons. For instance, if two countries wanted to make a treaty, the son of one king was often married to the daughter of the other king. After the wedding ceremony the children usually went back to live with their own parents until they were older.

HAVING A BABY. Babies were always born at home, because there were no hospitals. The lady in the picture above has three nurses to look after her. One is warming the new baby in front of the fire. Another child sleeps in the cradle. A nurse rocks the cradle by pulling the cord. Only rich families could afford a nurse. In poor families a neighbour came in to help the mother when her baby was born.

SWADDLING CLOTHES. Look at the picture above. You can see another nurse who is warming some material in front of the fire. These are the *swaddling clothes* which were wrapped tightly around all babies. The babies in the picture opposite are wearing swaddling clothes. People thought that wrapping a baby up like this gave him straight arms and legs.

BAPTISM. A baby was baptised, or christened, a few days after it was born. Our christening service is very like the medieval one. But there is one difference. When the medieval service was over, the priest told everyone to wash his hands before leaving the church. Otherwise he had to fast for forty days. Most people had no surnames—just Christian names. William became a popular boy's name after William of Normandy conquered England in 1066.

INFANT MORTALITY. Many babies died when they were very young. This is called *infant mortality*. They died because people did not understand the causes of illness and disease. There were hardly any doctors, and even they did not know much. People just didn't realize how important it was to be clean. Sick people often got worse because they lay in dirty beds, or drank medicine from dirty cups.

12

GIRLS. Most girls lived at home until they got married. Their mothers taught them how to cook, bake bread, spin thread, and make clothes. Sometimes, girls from rich families were sent to another family to learn good manners just as their brothers were. The three girls in the picture opposite are maids to the lady who is weaving cloth. They are combing and spinning the thread for her.

MAIDS. Below you can see another girl who has been sent to a noble household to be a maid. She is helping her mistress do her hair in plaits. Look at the comb—it has a row of teeth on both sides. Girls have used hair-dyes and make-up for hundreds of years. In 1265, during the reign of Henry III, a preacher called Philip told women off for "plastering their faces and dyeing their hair"!

COOKING. Food was cooked in big metal pots hung over open fires. The boy in the picture above is helping the cook by turning the metal spit on which meat is roasting. Notice how he is holding up a piece of wood to hide his face from the heat. Only lords and rich merchants had kitchens in their houses. Ordinary people cooked over the fire in their living room, like the family in the picture below.

BATHS. Not many people ever took a bath in the Middle Ages. Boys used to get quite violent when their mothers tried to wash them. "As soon as they have been washed they make themselves filthy dirty." Bath tubs were made of wood. When Edward II had a new bath tub built in Westminster Palace in 1315, the wood for it cost eight pence.

GARDENS. Most families had gardens, even if they lived in towns. But gardens were not just for children to play in. They were really meant for growing fruit and vegetables. As you can see in the picture opposite, children had to help look after the garden. In *Piers Plowman*, a popular story written about 1360, one garden produced beans, peas, leeks, parsley, shallots, onions, herbs, and half-ripe cherries. Perhaps the birds ate the ripe ones!

WEDDINGS. Here is a wedding between a young lady and an older man. If you think it looks different from weddings today, you are quite right. In the Middle Ages the most important part of the marriage service took place at the church door. Here, in front of the priest, the man and girl promised to be husband and wife. Then everyone went inside the church for the wedding mass.

18

Learning and Schools

Most children never went to school in the Middle Ages. Hardly any of them could read or write but, as there were very few books and no newspapers, this did not matter.

Boys who did attend school usually went to a song school, monastery school or grammar school. There were hardly any schools for girls. If a boy was clever and wanted to become a doctor or lawyer, he went to university as well.

Song schools were rather like Sunday schools today. The pupils learned to sing hymns and to read. Sometimes they were also taught to write. Spelling must have been very hard for them, because there were no rules. Only Latin words were spelled the same way each time. French and English words were spelled as each writer thought best. The boys at monastery schools usually became monks. Most medieval schoolboys went to grammar schools. Their teachers were clergymen and the schools were usually run by a monastery or church.

Discipline was very severe in all schools. When a Cambridge student received his Master of Arts degree he was given a birch cane and a *palmer*. He had to beat a small boy to show he could use them. The boy was paid two pence for his beating! The same Agnes Paston who beat her daughter hoped that her schoolboy son would "get truly lashed till he will amend (do better)."

MONASTERY SCHOOLS. These schools were run by the monks in their own monasteries. Boys who were going to be priests or monks when they grew up usually went to these schools. There was one teacher, an older monk, for every three or four boys. Above, a monk is teaching one boy while the others are reading. Notice that each boy has a book. Most books were hand-written by monks and monasteries had their own libraries.

GRAMMAR SCHOOLS. Most boys who went to school attended grammar schools, like the one in the picture opposite. These schools, as their name tells us, taught grammar, but not English grammar. Latin was the language that educated men used all over Europe. So the pupils had to learn Latin grammar. One teacher called grammar "the art of speaking and writing correctly, as do the writers of prose and poetry."

DISCIPLINE. Look at the pictures on the left. School discipline was very strict, and boys were caned even for little things. The teacher in the top picture is holding a birch cane. If the boy makes a mistake in his reading he will get a hard smack on his hand. Once, an Oxfordshire teacher called John de Neushom climbed into a willow tree to cut canes. But the poor man fell out of the tree into the river below, and was drowned.

OLDER STUDENTS. The older boys in the picture below will soon become priests or monks; we can tell this from their *tonsures*. Like all monks, the tops of their heads have been shaved so that hair only grows round the edges. These four students are having a lesson in logic, or the art of argument. The school master is testing the boy standing up by arguing with him. Logic was an important subject in every school.

WRITING. The teacher in the picture above is giving his pupils a writing lesson. You can tell he is a priest by his tonsure. These boys are very lucky to be learning how to write; most people in the Middle Ages could not write at all. That is why important documents had wax seals on them. Even if a king or nobleman could not write his name, he could stamp his seal or badge on the document.

PEN AND PARCHMENT. Paper was hard to get in the Middle Ages. Most monks and scholars wrote on *parchment* instead. Look at the pictures on the right. At the top, the writer is cutting a quill, or feather, pen with a special knife. Now you know how penknives get their name. On the stand in the picture below there is a pen in the inkpot. Writers also needed a lump of pumice to clean the parchment, a goat's tooth for polishing it, a ruler, and a rubber. There were no pencils or biros in those days!

NUMBERS. The lady in the left hand picture is showing her students how to use the new numbers. Why new? Because everyone used Roman numbers until the beginning of the 14th century. Big Ben has Roman numbers and so do most church clocks. These numbers did not make arithmetic very easy. Imagine trying to add XIV and LX! The numbers in this picture are called Arabic numerals. You can recognize some of the ones we still use today.

COMPASSES. These students are learning to draw squares, triangles and circles with compasses. The artist has probably made this picture up. How can we tell? Because ladies rarely taught in boys' schools. Only the older and more clever boys learned geometry. They probably studied it from a geometry book written by an English scholar called Adelard of Bath in the time of Henry I (1100–35).

WINCHESTER. In 1382 something important happened for English schooling. The Bishop of Winchester, William of Wykeham, founded a grammar school at Winchester. There were seventy pupils, which made it the biggest school in England. Even more important, it was not part of a cathedral or monastery; it was the first independent English school. Wykeham, whom you can see on the left, chose for his school the motto: "Manners Maketh Man." It shows how much people believed in politeness and courtesy in medieval times.

ETON. Sixty years later, in 1440, Henry VI copied Wykeham and founded a grammar school at Eton, shown in the picture below. Eton was the first school to be called a "public school". This meant that boys from all over England could go there. Before, children could only go to local schools. Both Eton and Winchester still use the old *medieval* buildings where boys have been studying for over five centuries.

EDUCATION FOR GIRLS. Very few girls went to school. If they did, it was usually to a convent school run by nuns. Here, girls learned to sew, to read a little, to sing, and perhaps to play a musical instrument. But most girls stayed at home. Rich men had private tutors for their sons, and sometimes let their daughters have lessons as well. The girl on the left probably had lessons with her brothers.

UNIVERSITY STUDENTS. In the Middle Ages, grammar schools and universities were much the same. Many university students were very young. Seventeen was the usual age to start at university, but many students were only thirteen or fourteen. There were no entrance exams. In fact, students who were slow at grammar could have special lessons to help them improve. Below you can see university students at a lecture.

UNIVERSITY TEACHING. *Theology* and law were mainly taught at university. Paris was the best place for theology. Law students usually went away to Bologna in Italy. A student had to stay at university for three years to become a Bachelor of Arts. But he didn't have to pass any exams at the end. He just had to prove to his teachers that he had been to enough lectures. How different from all our exams today!

GETTING A DEGREE. To become a Master of Arts, a student had to study for six years. He learned grammar, astronomy, music, geometry, logic, arithmetic and rhetoric. After six years, the student had a *disputation* with some of the university's cleverest men to show how much he had learned. He also had to invite his teachers to a banquet. He then got his degree, and the cap of a Master of Arts like the student in the picture opposite. He was also given a rod to beat his own pupils.

33

34

OXFORD UNIVERSITY. William of Wykeham also founded New College at Oxford. On the left you can see William with some of the College's staff and students. In the background are the chapel, and the hall used for lectures and meals. Oxford was famous for learning as early as Henry I's reign. In 1315 the university had more than 1,000 students. Cambridge was a famous university, too. Continental scholars came to England to study at Oxford and Cambridge.

TOWN AND GOWN. Students have always been known for their high spirits and noisy behaviour. Medieval students often wore swords, and got into many bad fights. The students below are arguing with some older men. Notice that one is already holding his sword. In 1209, during King John's reign, there was so much trouble between townsmen and students in Oxford that all the students had to leave. But many years later in a great riot, the students soundly defeated the apprentices and townspeople.

Page, Squire and Knight

Rich families thought that learning good manners was more important than learning to read and write. When a boy was about eight or nine years old, he was sent to the house of another nobleman to become a *page*, along with several other boys. They all played and studied together, and became well-mannered young men. Girls from noble families were sometimes sent away to be maids or ladies-in-waiting, but this was not very common.

Many books about good manners were written in the Middle Ages. One of these was *The Babees' Book*. It was written in 1475, probably for Edward and Richard, the two Princes in the Tower. It was a very long book, full of "do's" and "don'ts". Children must never stuff their mouths too full at mealtimes; they were not to pick their noses or teeth; nor should they bite their nails. When the lord came into the room they must stand up straight and not "jangle" (chatter).

An Italian called Trevisano visited England in 1497, during Henry VII's reign. He asked why parents sent their children away to be brought up in strange houses. "The children learn better manners in other people's houses," he was told. But he was still horrified by this custom.

PAGES. Small boys, like the two in the picture below, were sent to the homes of noblemen as part of their education. At these big houses and castles they acted as pages to a knight or a *squire*. In the days before electric light, people "got up with the sun." A page had to be up even earlier; he had to help his lord wash and dress.

TABLE MANNERS. Banquets were very popular in medieval times, and every page needed to learn good table manners. It was very rude to gnaw bones. Dipping food in the salt bowl, which everyone shared, was even worse. This was probably a good thing, because medieval people ate with their fingers and did not bother to wash their hands.

WAITING AT TABLE. Young pages also learned how to serve at table. It was a great honour to wait on important people. These boys on the left are bringing in fish for the king and his guests. Notice that there are no forks or spoons on the table, only knives. Forks were not really used until the 16th century. Many older people disliked them and thought they were "new-fangled".

CARVING. If he had been a good page, a boy became a squire when he reached his teens. Every squire had to be able to carve meat well. The Squire in Geoffrey Chaucer's *Canterbury Tales* "carved before his father at table." It was an honour to carve at the dining table, so he must have been good at it. A squire had to carve cooked oxen, deer, swans, and peacocks, as well as the meat and poultry we eat today.

CAROLES. Pages and squires were expected to sing and dance well. As early as the 12th century, Welsh people were famous for their singing. English people enjoyed their *caroles*. These combined both singing and dancing and were very popular at holiday times. The English were well-known for their caroles, even in Europe. Morris dancing is all that remains of our many medieval dances.

WRITING. Noblemen's sons had to learn to ride, hawk and dance. It did not really matter if they could not read or write. Some rich men hired tutors to teach their sons and pages. The boys opposite are writing on strips of parchment laid over their knees. It doesn't look very comfortable!

HAWKING.   Hawking, or falconry, was a favourite
sport among noblemen. A page learned how to
hawk by going out with hunting parties from the
castle. At first he was only allowed to hold the hounds.
He let them loose when the fierce falcon brought
down its prey. Then he had many months of practice
with the hawks. At last, one proud day, he could carry
a falcon on his own gloved fist. Above, you see two
men training a falcon, using a lure that looks like a bird.

ARCHERY. Archers were the most important part of every medieval army. Arrows could even pierce the armour worn by a knight or his horse. However brave a knight, he was useless if his horse was brought down by an arrow. The archers in William of Normandy's army helped to defeat the Saxons at the Battle of Hastings in 1066. All boys learned to shoot with a bow and arrow. In 1365, during Edward III's reign, a law was made punishing any man or boy who did not practise archery every Sunday.

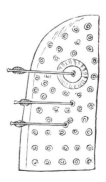

SWORD PRACTICE. The ambition of every nobleman's son was to become a knight. But boys first
had to learn to use simple weapons. Little boys played
with wooden swords and shields. They learned the
hard way how to dodge blows and hit back. As they
grew older they practised with metal weapons, until
they were ready to fight with the huge swords and
shields of the men.

TILTING. Squires who had learned to ride well and
to use a sword were taught how to *tilt* at a *quintain*.
Tilting was a way of practising for battle. The squire,
wearing armour, mounted his horse and charged—
just as you see in the picture below. As he hit the
shield with his long blunt lance, the heavy weight at
the other end of the bar swung up. If the rider did
not dodge the blow. he was knocked off his horse.

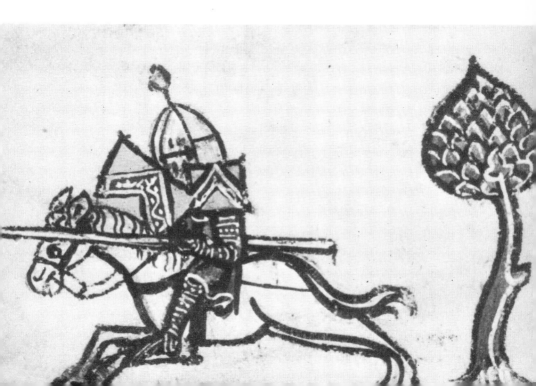

TOURNAMENTS. Early in the Middle Ages *tourna-ments* were very popular among noblemen. Two nobles each got together a group of armed and mounted knights. At a signal, the two groups charged each other from opposite ends of a field. In the free-for-all that followed many were actually killed. But the idea was really to capture, not to kill. A captured knight had to pay a ransom to get free.

JOUSTS. Tournaments turned into *jousting* matches. These were not so rough and dangerous. Edward III organized many jousts, and they became very popular. When heralds sounded their trumpets, two mounted knights charged at each other. Each tried to knock the other off his horse. Later, a barrier was set up between the knights. People thought this made the joust dull, because it stopped head-on collisions.

KNIGHTS. Of course, every page and squire hoped to become a knight. He wanted to wear a coat of armour like the knight shown above and ride a fine horse. But all this was very expensive. During the reigns of Edward III and Richard II, well-trained war horses cost £100 each. It is hard to compare this amount with our money, but it was probably like buying a Rolls Royce today. There were never many more than 400 knights in England at any one time.

RECEIVING A KNIGHTHOOD. A squire could become a knight only if he or his father owned lands which could be rented for more than £15 each year. This does not sound like much. But in Edward III's time, a ploughman only got 67p for a whole year's work! To him £15 was a fortune. This soldier is being knighted on the battlefield. Only men who had shown great bravery in battle had this honour.

Apprentices
and Journeymen

When a boy reached his teens, his parents usually apprenticed him to a master-craftsman for about seven years. In this way he learned a trade or craft, so that he could earn his living when he grew up. Just as noblemen's sons went to live in the homes of other rich men to learn good behaviour, an apprentice had to live at the home of the master-craftsman who was teaching him.

Each trade and craft had its own *guild*. The guilds looked after their members and made rules about hours of work and holidays. They checked the quality of the goods, and handled complaints from the public. If a guild member did bad work or cheated a customer, he was punished by the guild court. In 1419, during Henry V's reign, a London coal-merchant had to stand in the *pillory* for a day, because he had sold lightweight sacks of coal.

When an apprentice had finished his seven years, he had to prove to the guild officials that he was good at his trade. He made something special, like a fancy coat if he was a tailor, or a piece of furniture if he was a carpenter, to show off his skill. It was called his "master-piece." If it was a good piece of work he was allowed to call himself a master-craftsman and start his own business. But it was expensive to start a business, and many apprentices worked as *journeymen*. There were always many journeymen in medieval towns.

APPRENTICE BUILDERS. The building trade employed many different kinds of workers. Above, masons are building a wall, as a king looks on. Perhaps they are building him a castle. The boy climbing the ladder is an apprentice. Apprentices had to do all the hard, dull jobs before they could learn to lay bricks or carve stone.

MORE BUILDERS. The apprentice in the picture opposite carries cement to the mason working on the walls. Look at the scaffolding they are using. It is wooden, with cane matting to stand on. Do you think it is safe? The man in the front is cutting and shaping the stone blocks. During Edward I's reign (1272–1307), the masons building Merton College in Oxford were paid 8½p a week.

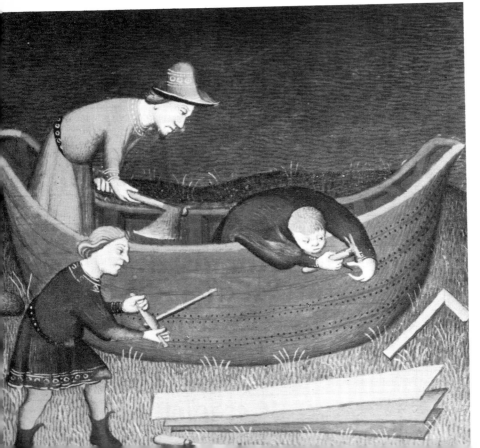

SCULPTORS. The great cathedrals and churches built in medieval times were decorated with carved stone figures. You can see the fine carvings around the great west doors of Salisbury and Wells cathedrals and on the cathedrals of Amiens and Rheims in France. The pictures above show a stone-carver's apprenticeship. First he shapes plain building blocks. Next he learns to make decorative stones for pillars. After many years, he is finally allowed to carve the statues.

SHIPBUILDERS. Shipping was the cheapest form of transport. The rivers and sea coasts in England and on the Continent were always filled with boats. All boats were made of wood. These apprentices on the left are hammering iron nails to hold the wooden planks together. Even in those days customs duties had to be paid on all goods arriving at a port. For example, at Southampton during Henry III's reign (1461–83), John Aport, had to pay £6 on three sacks of hemp.

Image labels: ərcac in, folles, igi, malleũ·, incudis, ferrarij duo dem cenc ferrum·

BLACKSMITHS. Blacksmiths were skilled and busy men. In the villages they made and mended farm tools, and shod horses. They even repaired weapons and armour. A Norfolk landlord paid his blacksmith £1 and three sacks of wheat a year. This was a good wage, and parents liked their sons to become blacksmiths. Above is a blacksmith's forge, with its fire and bellows. The two apprentices are learning how to beat a piece of hot metal into shape.

ARMOURERS. These two armourers and their young apprentices are resting after a day's work. Every nobleman had at least one armourer at his castle to make all the coats of armour for his knights. In 1298 the armourer's forge at Berwick Castle had three troughs for water, three anvils, six pairs of pincers, six pairs of bellows, two great hammers, one great anvil and pickaxe and one little one. An apprentice armourer had a lot to learn.

COOPERS. In the Middle Ages all liquids were carried in barrels. It was hard to make barrels that did not leak. Barrel-makers were called *coopers*. The surname "Cooper" comes from this word. The master-craftsman on the right, who is wearing a hat, shapes the planks or staves for the barrels. His apprentice is making the metal bands to keep the staves in place. The two journeymen at the back are finishing a barrel.

NAIL-MAKERS. These apprentices are heating iron in the fire so they can shape it into nails. There was an old saying: "For lack of a nail a shoe was lost, for lack of a shoe a horse was lost, for lack of a horse a rider was lost, for lack of a rider a battle was lost—and all for the lack of a horseshoe nail."

PAPERMAKERS. Spanish craftsmen at Valencia and Toledo were making paper a long time ago, in the year 1150. The picture opposite shows a papermaker and his apprentice. The watermill you see through the window beats rotten cloth and linen to a pulp. The craftsman puts this pulp into shallow moulds, which are placed in the vat to make wet spongy sheets. The boy carries a tray of these sheets to the screw press behind his master.

SHOEMAKERS. The picture below comes from a stained glass window in Rouen Cathedral, France. The boy is a shoemaker's apprentice. He is busy working on his master-piece. He must show the guild that he can make all kinds of shoes before he is allowed to become a master-craftsman. The shoemakers' guild had strict rules. Members could make shoes, but they could not mend them. That was the cobblers' job.

WEAVERS. Small children often helped their parents at work. This is a family of weavers from *Hainault*. When King Edward III married Philippa of Hainault in 1328 many of these weavers came to England. They helped to make the English cloth industry well-known all over Europe. These two weavers below are working together, so they can make a wide piece of cloth. It was called broadcloth; it was about 5 feet wide and 72 feet long.

CLOTH MERCHANTS. Below is a cloth merchant's shop. Most people bought cloth and made their own clothes. If they were rich, they paid a tailor to make clothes for them. There were no ready-made clothes in those days. Many cloth shops also employed one or two tailors. They made clothes from the material a customer bought. This boy and girl are learning the tailor's trade.

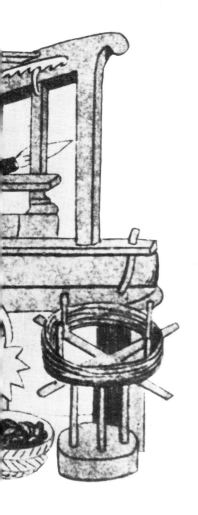

MASTERPIECES. The two boys in the picture opposite have finished their seven years' apprenticeship. To show they have learned their crafts well, they are making their master-pieces. They are watched by a guild official. The boy on the left is carving stone. He is a stone mason. On the right is an apprentice carpenter. Our word master-piece comes from this medieval practice. A master-piece is a very good piece of work.

INDUSTRIAL DISPUTES. Industrial disputes and wage claims are not new. They even happened in the Middle Ages. When apprentices became journeymen, they often complained about their wages. Perhaps this group of journeymen are arguing about their pay. Many people died during the *Black Death* of 1348–49. With the shortage of workmen, they could demand higher wages. So Edward III passed a law in 1350 called the Statute of Labourers. This law fixed everyone's wages. For example, a carpenter was to be paid twopence a day and a housemaid a penny a week.

Country Children

Rich boys learned to read and write, to ride horses and hunt; town boys became apprentices and learned a craft. But what about country children? In the Middle Ages, more people lived in the country than in towns. How did all these children spend their time?

Most country people were *villeins*. Some villeins were craftsmen. Each village had its carpenter, blacksmith, and wheelwright. These men were often quite well paid. In 1366 a blacksmith could earn £1 a year, but a ploughman only got 66p and a shepherd 50p.

But these craftsmen were few. Most villeins did farmwork for their landlord. For two or three days each week, villeins had to work for their lord— ploughing and sowing in the spring, haymaking and harvesting in the summer. On the other days they were free to cultivate their own strips of land.

Villeins were often very poor, and found it hard to make a living. They had to grow all their own food, spin thread and weave cloth. Everyone in the family was expected to help. As soon as a boy was strong enough to manage a plough, he ploughed the lord's lands. This gave the father more time to work on the family's own fields. Little girls learned to look after the chickens and to collect the eggs. Later, they helped their mothers to churn butter and weave cloth.

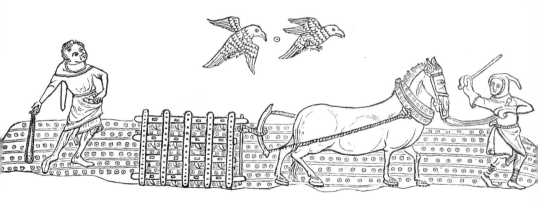

BIRD SCARING. Birds stole much of the seed planted each year in the spring. Scaring the birds away was one of the first things a boy did to help his family. Small boys just shouted or threw stones at the birds. But older boys, like the one above, used slings and stones. If they knocked down a fat pigeon or rook, it made a good supper for the family.

THE BAILIFF. The landlord's *bailiff* is having a word with this young farm worker in the picture opposite. Notice that the boy has taken off his hat and holds it in his hand. It was very bad manners for any child to wear a hat when talking to someone in authority. The bailiff ran the lord's estate. He told the villeins what to do, and made sure they carried out his orders. Here he tells the boy what to do next.

BIRD SNARING. Children made a little money for their families by snaring birds to sell as pets. Many rich people kept caged birds, just as we keep budgies today. The brightly coloured bullfinches and gold-finches were very popular with ladies. They also kept magpies and taught them to talk. In 1387 the Bishop of Winchester had to stop the nuns bringing their birds into church!

SHEPHERDS. The artist, possibly a monk, who painted this picture shows us a typical English country scene in the time of Edward II. A shepherd had to be out with his flock in all weathers. Boys often helped to mind the sheep. The shepherd is helped by his sons. One son tends a lamb, the other has his bagpipes in his lap.

SWINEHERDS. Every family had a few pigs, and young boys usually looked after them. In the autumn when the nuts on the trees were ripe, the village boys herded all the pigs into the woods. The boys knocked the nuts off the trees with sticks and stones, just like the boy in this picture above. The pigs got very fat eating all the nuts. When winter came each family killed all its pigs. The pork was salted and provided the family with enough meat for the winter.

HARVEST. It was not only men who did farm work. Women and girls helped, too. Autumn was a very busy time and the whole family worked in the fields harvesting the crops. This mother in the picture opposite is bringing lunch to her husband and daughter who have been working since daylight. The men cut the corn and the girls tie it into bundles. On the left you can see a cart load going to the barn for storage.

EVR
LVXEMBÓVRG

AN·DNI·1463·

LE COTE DE
CHAR ROLLÓIS
ET
ADAME DE BOVRBON

BA

B

Holidays, Sports and Entertainments

Medieval people did not have long annual holidays But they did not work every day, all the year round. The Church was very powerful in the Middle Ages, and it ordered that no one should work on Sundays. The Church also named special days as saints' days, and these were holidays, too. Did you know that our word holiday comes from medieval times? In those days it was spelt "holyday", because Sundays and saints' days were holy. As the years passed holy days became fewer, but the word stuck, and a holiday, like a holy day, is still a day off work.

Holidays were times of fun and gaiety. Children who lived in the Middle Ages enjoyed them as much as we do today. Because houses were quite small, there were many street entertainments and outdoor games.

Fairs grew out of these holidays. Everyone had to go to church on a saint's day. The day of the parish church's special, or patron saint, was a big occasion. All the villagers came to the service in a gay, happy mood. A clever man put up a stall to sell pies and ale. The villagers liked this idea and put up more stalls to sell other goods. As the years went by, more people came and more stalls were built. The fair grew into a big event and everyone forgot the saint whose day had started it all. The famous Bartholomew Fair at Smithfield in London, on August 24th, began in this way.

BALL GAMES. As there are so many round things in nature, balls are probably the oldest toys in the world. Apples, oranges, coconuts—all make good balls. The schoolboys in the picture above are playing hand-ball during a break from their lessons. In the background you can see two masters having a game of chess. Below, a brother and sister are playing bowls in the garden.

BATS AND BALLS. Children in the Middle Ages liked to play with bats and balls, too. Older boys and men played club ball, as you can see in the top picture. Apprentices and students played a sort of hockey. There was no special pitch, and very few rules. The teams played out in the streets. The games were so rough and noisy that they were banned in Westminster when Parliament was sitting, because the noise disturbed the Members!

SPINNING TOPS. Many of the toys and games we have today are very old. The painting opposite of boys spinning a top comes from a medieval prayer book. Other pictures show us that boys in the Middle Ages played with toy soldiers, and their sisters with dolls. Edward I, who ruled England from 1272 to 1307, enjoyed giving toys to his children, such as small bows and arrows, or a model cart.

JOUSTING GAMES. Children often copy grown-ups in their games. These boys are not big enough to ride real horses and joust in real tournaments like their fathers. Instead they play at jousting. They "ride" wooden hobby-horses. Their "weapons" are funny looking lances, with something rather like a windmill at the end. One day, perhaps, they will fight in real tournaments.

BOBBING THE APPLE. Children were not the only ones to play games in medieval times; grown-ups enjoyed them, too. Blindman's-bluff, or hoodman-blind as it was called then, was a grown-up's game. People liked to play it during the long dark winter evenings. Bobbing the apple was also popular with adults. The players had to catch a hanging apple in their teeth without using their hands.

CHESS. The rich liked to play chess. Chess started
in the Far East and became popular in Europe about
the time of the Norman Conquest in 1066. Both boys
and girls were taught to play chess. Young men
learned to play the game when they were squires.
A popular story of Edward I's reign tells us that squires
liked to entertain the ladies of the house by playing
chess with them.

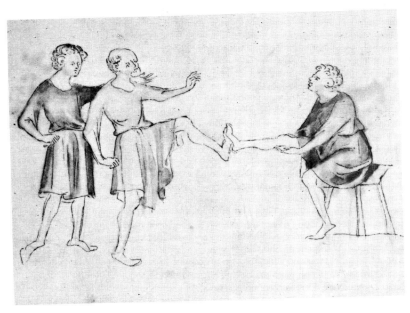

WRESTLING. Look at the pictures on the left. Wrestling matches were a highlight of every holiday. Clerkenwell, just outside the walls of London, was famous for its wrestling. The crowds were so large that they trampled all the crops in nearby fields. The head of the nunnery which owned the fields complained to King Edward I about it. Foot-fighting was less common, but people enjoyed it. They put bets on who would win.

BEAR-BAITING. Many sports of the Middle Ages seem cruel to us now. Bear-baiting was one such sport. A bear was chained to a post and dogs were made to attack it. The bear often killed a few dogs at first. But finally the bear became so tired that the dogs killed it.

COCK FIGHTING. Cockfighting was another cruel, but popular sport. Two cocks were forced to attack each other until one was killed. Schoolboys had their own version of this game. A bird was tied to a post by its foot or beak. The boys took turns to throw stones at it until it was killed.

PERFORMING ANIMALS. Children in the Middle Ages liked to watch animals that could do tricks. Some men earned their living travelling from one fair to another with performing animals. Monkeys learn tricks easily, and they were great favourites with the crowds. The picture below was drawn in the reign of Henry III. The artist drew what he saw, so the monkeys must have worn little clothes. But do you think they *really* played their instruments?

ACROBATS AND JUGGLERS. Street acrobats and jugglers were always sure of a good audience. Families toured England and the Continent with their acts. As soon as a child was old enough to juggle a few balls, he joined in. Girl acrobats usually entertained guests at royal feasts. Some courts had a jester. He was paid to be funny, rather like our comedians today. St. Bartholomew's Hospital, London, was founded by Rahere, the jester to Henry I.

MAY DAY. Everyone looked forward to May Day. It was a day for feasting and dancing. People knew that winter was really over, and that summer was on its way. The girls on the right are picking spring flowers to make into wreaths and garlands. The girl on the left is placing one on her head. Soon they will go and join their friends in the May Day dancing.

DANCING. A holiday was not a holiday without
dancing. People loved to dance, but clergymen often
gave sermons against it. In 1223, the Bishop of
Salisbury stopped all dancing in the churchyards.
That seems a strange place to have a dance! Children
learned to dance when they were very young. In
some ways, medieval boys and girls were much like
children today. Do you think you would have liked to
have grown up in the Middle Ages?

Table of Dates

1066	Duke William of Normandy defeats King Harold at the Battle of Hastings and becomes William I
1085–86	William I orders a survey of England to be carried out. The result was the Domesday Book
c.1150	Papermills are built in Spain
1200	Coal is exported from Newcastle to the Continent
1215	King John seals the Great Charter
1265	Representatives of the big towns attend the English Parliament; the beginning of the House of Commons
1348–49	Thousands of people die from the Black Death
1350	Edward III passes the Statute of Labourers to fix wages
1382	William of Wykeham founds Winchester School
1387–90	Geoffrey Chaucer writes the *Canterbury Tales*
1440	Henry VI founds Eton College
1478	William Caxton prints the first book in English
1485	Henry Tudor defeats Richard III at the Battle of Bosworth and becomes Henry VII, the first Tudor king

New Words

Bailiff	Man in charge of a lord's estate
Black Death	Bubonic plague which killed thousands of people in England and Europe
Carole	Country dance combining singing and dancing
Cooper	A barrel-maker
Disputation	A learned argument held by students
Guild	An association of merchants or craftsmen in the same trade or craft
Hainault	A small independent state in what is now south-west Belgium
Infant mortality	The death of babies and small children
Journeymen	Skilled workmen hired and paid by the day. The word comes from the French word *journée,* a day
Jousting	Mock fight between two armed and mounted knights
Medieval	A word used to describe people and things of the Middle Ages
Middle Ages	The period roughly between 1066 and 1500
Page	Young boy from a noble family training to become a knight

Palmer	Stick with a wooden disk, used to smack children's hands
Parchment	Material made from sheepskin, used for writing on
Pillory	Wooden post with a hole in it. Offenders had their heads clamped in the hole
Quintain	Post with a shield on it. Knights and squires practised fighting by charging at the shield
Squire	Young man who had learned his duties as a page and now serves a knight
Swaddling clothes	Long strips of material in which babies were wrapped
Theology	The study of the Bible and religion
Tilting	Charging on horseback at a mounted opponent or at the quintain
Tonsure	The shaving of the top of a monk's head
Tournament	Mock fight between two bands of knights
Villein	Medieval peasant who farmed land for his landlord

More Books

Davies, P. *Town Life in the Middle Ages* (Wayland, 1972). Another book in this series.

Davies, P. *Country Life in the Middle Ages* (Wayland, 1972). Another book in this series.

Duggan, A. *Growing up in the Thirteenth Century* (Faber, 1962). A good picture of medieval childhood. For older readers.

Hindley, G. *Medieval Warfare* (Wayland, 1971). Contains hundreds of detailed pictures, many in colour.

Mitchell, R. J. *The Medieval Feast* (Longman, 1958). A clear account of an important occasion.

Neurath, M. *They Lived Like This in Chaucer's England* (Max Parrish, 1967). Good descriptions of the lives of different people at the time.

Reeves, M. *The Medieval Town* (Longman, 1966). Compare this with the *The Medieval Village* by the same author, to see how people lived.

Sutcliffe, R. *The Armourer's House* (O.U.P., 1966). A vivid story of a child's life in late medieval times.

Sutcliffe, R. *Knights Fee* (O.U.P., 1966). The exciting story of how a boy became a knight in Norman England. Probably best for older boys.

Trease, G. *Bows against the Barons* (Brockhampton Press, 1966). England's most famous outlaw, Robin Hood, and his fight against the barons.

Index

Picture Credits

The Publishers wish to thank the following for their kind permission to reproduce copyright illustrations on the pages mentioned: Trustees of the British Museum, jacket, frontispiece, 6, 11, 12, 13, 16, 17, 20, 21, 22 (top), 23, 24, 25, 26, 27, 30, 31, 35, 36, 38, 40, 41, 46, 47, 48, 49, 52, 54, 55, 57 (bottom), 58–59, 60–61, 67, 68, 70, 73 (bottom), 75, 78, 80–81, 84, 88, 89; Radio-Times Hulton Picture Library, 18, 22 (bottom), 32, 33, 43, 64; Mansell Collection, 28 (top), 56–57, 61 (top), 66, 87 (top); National Monuments Record, 28–29; Trustees of the Victoria and Albert Museum, 83; Bibliotheque Nationale, 51. Other illustrations appearing in this book are the property of the Wayland Picture Library.